SPRING VOLUME

MICHIGAN
Wildflowers
UP CLOSE AND PERSONAL

Dr. Dee Howe

PenCraft Books

Published by PenCraft Books, LLC

ISBN: 978-1-939556-22-6 (Print)

First published: March, 2017 USA

Published by: PenCraft Books LLC,
7348 Maple Terrace, Traverse City, MI 49686, USA

CONTENTS

Melissa,
may nature's beauty
enrich your life.

DEDICATION

This book is dedicated to the memory of Mrs. Irons, a 4-H volunteer who shared her passion of Michigan wildflowers with a small group of Daly School kids many years ago.

INTRODUCTION

This book has developed over a span of fifty years, since I was first introduced to Michigan Wildflowers in a 4-H club in Hesperia, charged with the task of locating and identifying fifty local wildflowers. My response, "Impossible-there aren't that many in the whole state of Michigan!!" Over the years the count has risen from that original fifty to over two hundred and fifty, and there are more yet to discover. It has been an amazing journey so far, tramping through woods and fields, sinking into bogs, wading around lake and river edges, and lying in every kind of terrain imaginable to get the perfect shot.

Along this journey I have shared the love of Michigan wildflowers with my parents, Joe and Neva Barr, who spent hours exploring the woods with me; with my children, Kelli, Lisa, and Tony, and with my grandchildren, Maddi, Nathan, Lucy, and Laney, who love to explore and learn with Mom and Grandma.

There have been pivotal people that have made this book a reality: Dave Littell, who mentored me with my first Nikon and encouraged me to always get closer to the flowers; Tom Schneider, who took an interest in a recent photo display, listened to why this book was at a standstill, and found a solution; and to David Case, company president of Fox Portrait Studios, Roseville, and Radu Magureanu, company controller, for providing digital scans from film that surpassed my expectations.

The last fifteen years have been the most prolific time in my wildflower search as I've had more time to spend with my camera in the woods. My best friend, Bill Hamilton, has walked many, many miles with me over these last fifteen years. He has driven numerous dirt roads as I hung out the passenger window to catch a glimpse of color. He has kept track of how to get back to civilization as I wandered off wooded pathways. He has pulled me out of bogs. He has assisted with crutches when I had my eye on a new discovery and failed to watch where I was walking. He has transported many framed photos to displays around Michigan. It is due to his constant encouragement and his belief that my photos are more than just a hobby, that the negatives in the closet have become Michigan Wildflowers: Up Close and Personal.

Bloodroot
Poppy Family

aka Sweet Slumber

The Bloodroot can be located as early as March in rich woodlands, along streams, or in wet areas, just as the snow is receding and the soil begins to thaw. When the leaf appears, it is wrapped around the flower stem which grows to a height of five to ten inches.

The Bloodroot closes each night until it is pollinated, then the petals drop, still looking as though they are new petals. Within a few weeks a long seed pod develops.

The Bloodroot does not produce nectar, but the seed has a fleshy white band that is eaten by ants as they disperse the seeds.

As the name suggests, a break in the stem or the root causes a reddish orange juice to flow. This juice was used by Native Americans for clothing dye, war paint, and insect repellent. Applying the juice to skin is not safe as this plant is toxic and can kill skin tissue.

Blue Cohosh
Barberry Family

aka Papoose Root, Squaw Root, Blue Berry, Blueberry Root

The Blue Cohosh flower is an inconspicuous one half inch, yellow green flower, and can be found in shady, moist, deciduous woods beginning in April. The small flowers begin to open while the leaves are still folded. The clusters of up to twenty flowers can be found atop a stem about two feet high. This stem in spring is purplish blue and appears to be covered with a white dust.

The Blue Cohosh has three to five lobes on each leaflet, which differ slightly between the plants that have flowers and those that don't. Deer tend to avoid this plant due to the bitter taste of the foliage.

The poisonous dark blue berries found later in the summer reflect the name Blue Cohosh. One use of this plant by Native Americans was to relieve pain in childbirth, which may have led to some of the alternate names.

Blue Flag
Iris Family

*aka Blue Iris, Northern Iris, Flag Lily, Water Flag,
Poison Flag*

The Blue Flag can be seen in wet, swampy areas
such as marshes, and ditches along the roadside,
beginning in May.

This two to four-inch flower atop stiff two to three
foot stalks appears similar to other Iris species at
a distance; however, the white on the petal, the
yellow throat, and the dark colored veins are
unique to the Blue Flag.

The word flag (middle English flagge) means
"reed," referring to the long narrow leaves.

Blue Toadflax

Figwort Family

aka Old-field Toadflax

The Blue Toadflax is found beginning in late April in full sun areas of sandy or rocky soil. Only a few of the flowers bloom simultaneously, so the blooming period of a colony can last two to three months.

The foliage on this six to twenty-four inch plant is wispy, with long narrow leaves at the base.

Due to the long thin spur which protrudes from each flower, long tongued bees, such as bumblebees, are required to pollinate this plant.

Bluebead Lily
Lily Family

aka Bluebead, Yellow Clintonia, Corn Lily

The Bluebead Lily is usually found in May in moist woods with high acid content. The three to six yellowish green bells, which are about one inch long, are grouped on the top of a six to ten inch leafless stalk. The leaves of the Bluebead Lily, which grow on separate stems, are unique in that they are thick and fleshy, and when broken, ooze a clear fluid which smells like cucumbers.

The name Bluebead comes from the true blue color of poisonous berries, which may be found at the end of the summer.

A similar species, White Clintonia, has white flowers and black berries and is considered rare.

Blue-eyed Grass

Iris Family

aka Star Grass

Blue-eyed Grass is not a true grass, but is found in meadows and low woods in May amongst other tall grasses. The stem is flat and twisted, usually branched, and can be as tall as eighteen inches.

The leaves of the Blue-eyed Grass are very thin and as tall as the stem. The flower itself is only a half inch wide, but with all the characteristics of the Iris Family.

Native Americans used root tea for diarrhea and plant tea for stomachaches and laxatives.

Two species of Blue-eyed Grass are found in Michigan: the Pointed Blue-eyed Grass and the Common Blue-eyed Grass, which differ by the width of the leaves and the branched or unbranched stems.

Blue-eyed Mary
Figwort Family

The Blue-eyed Mary self-seeds, which leads to large colonies in moist, open woods and stream sides. This bi-colored flower, which is smaller than a thumbnail, grows on weak stems up to fifteen inches tall beginning the end of April.

Only insects with long tongues can collect nectar from the Blue-eyed Mary due to the unique structure of the third lobe of the lower lip. This lobe is folded lengthwise and hangs below the other two blue petals encasing the stamens and style making it difficult for insects to reach.

Blue-eyed Mary is a threatened species in Michigan, but may still be found in the southeastern corner of the state.

Bunchberry
Dogwood Family

aka Crackerberry, Canadian Dogwood, Dwarf Dogwood, Ground Dogwood

The Bunchberry is only three to eight inches tall, making it the smallest plant of the Dogwood Family. It begins to bloom the end of April on conifer forest floors.

Although the flower appears to be a four-petal white flower, these are actually the bracts that surround the tiny one eighth inch green flowers in the center. These tiny flowers form into a tight bunch of red berries later in the summer.

The Bunchberry has an exploding pollen mechanism[1] that is triggered by flying insects. The pollen sticks to the insect's body and is transferred to other flowers.

---

1 The tiny flowers have been timed and explode open in less the ½ millisecond, the fastest movement recorded in a plant (dsc.discovery.com/news/briefs/20050509/fastplant.html).

Canada Mayflower

Lily Family

aka False Lily-of-the-Valley Wild, Lily-of-the-Valley, Snakeberry, Deerberry, Deer Heart, May Lily

The Canada Mayflower is first found in May in shaded conifer or deciduous woods, and along streams, in large mats of one to three inch leaves. It is considered an invader as it spreads so quickly.

The tiny star shaped one eighth inch flowers form creamy cylinder shaped flower heads atop a three to six inch zigzag stem with two to three heart shaped leaves.

Although the Canada Mayflower is part of the Lily Family, the flower parts are in twos: two petals, two sepals, and four stamens. Other flowers in the Lily Family have three petals, three sepals, and six stamens.

Canada Violet

Violet Family

aka Canadian White Violet

The Canada Violet is distinguished from other white violets by the purple tint on the back of the upper petals, and the dark purple veins on the lower petals.

This native plant is found late April and early May in moist woodlands and forests growing eight to sixteen inches high, with the flower measuring no more than one inch across.

The Canada Violet leaves are heart shaped, pointed, finely toothed, and shiny, with the leaves and flowers on the same stalk. This is one of the few violets that have a pleasant scent.

The seed capsules split open explosively, and shoot out browning seeds to form colonies of plants.

Columbine

Buttercup Family

The Columbine, with drooping red and yellow flowers, is easily found in April and May in open areas due to its height and coloring.

The five long curved spurs contain the nectar, but only a few pollinators, such as the hummingbird and long-tongued moths, can reach the nectar. Some insects do bite the end of the spur and suck the nectar out that way.

Many gardeners plant domesticated Columbines of various colors to attract hummingbirds, but this is the only color of the native plant.

Common Buttercup

Buttercup Family

aka Tall Buttercup, Meadow Buttercup

Beginning in May, the Common Buttercup is found in fields and meadows. It is similar to the more often seen Swamp Buttercup that grows by streams.

This native of Europe is two to three feet high, the tallest of the Buttercup Family, and its stem is erect, hairy, and branching.

The one inch cup shaped blossom has a distinctive waxy texture caused by a special layer of cells just beneath the surface cells.

The Common Buttercup is avoided by livestock due to poisoning, and therefore spreads rapidly.

Common Speedwell

Figwort Family

The Common Speedwell is a spike of tiny one fourth inch wide flowers which open starting at the bottom of the two to six inch stem. Each flower is composed of four petals, with the lowest one being the narrowest, and the other three streaked with dark blue. The petals are sometimes white, and sometimes a pale blue.

The Common Speedwell can be found beginning in May, along roadsides, in meadows, in damp open woods, and in lawns.

Common Strawberry

Rose Family

aka Beach Strawberry

The Common Strawberry, with its typical rose structure of five rounded sepals and petals, surrounding a dome-like structure, is found in early spring in open fields and woods. These domes soon turn into sweet wild strawberries, richer than most domestic species. In fact, this species is the original parent of 90 percent of all the cultivated strawberries now grown.

This perennial spreads by producing long runners that root at the nodes, making new plants. Both the fruit, and the leaves which are often used to make tea, are high in vitamin C.

Another strawberry also found in May in open fields is the Indian Strawberry, introduced from India; however, the flowers of the Indian Strawberry are a bright yellow and the fruit is tasteless.

Crested Dwarf Iris
Iris Family

aka Dwarf Crested Iris

The Crested Dwarf Iris is only about two inches wide and grows on a short slender stem four to nine inches tall. The leaves surrounding the flower are narrow and pointed, and about four to ten inches long. The Crested Dwarf Iris is found on wooded hillsides and ravines in May, and is attractive to hummingbirds and bees.

Each seedling takes up to three years to flower, and although it appears fragile, the Crested Dwarf Iris can live up to ten years.

The yellow or white "beard" distinguishes this flower from the Dwarf Iris.

Cut-leaved Toothwort

Mustard Family

The Cut-leaved Toothwort is one of the early flowers of spring found in rich moist deciduous woods. It stands about ten inches tall, with a loose cluster of three to fifteen white, pink, or lavender flowers atop the stem. Each four petal flower is about three fourths inch wide.

The whorled leaves are two to five inches wide, deeply divided, and sharply toothed. The underground stems have tooth-like projections. These two characteristics suggest the name of this plant.

This perennial plant is a host plant for the Checkered White Butterfly caterpillar.

Dame's Rocket
Mustard Family

aka Sweet Rocket, Dame's Violet, Mother-of-the-Evening

The showy clusters of three fourths inch purple or white flowers known as Dame's Rocket begin to bloom in mid-April. Although often confused with varieties of Phlox, counting the petals will assist with identification; Dame's Rocket has four petals, and Phlox has five petals.

The four foot high stem, and its leaves, are covered with fine hairs, and grow in well drained soil in full sun or partial shade. In the evening the Dame's Rocket gives off a stronger odor than the light, pleasant fragrance found during the day.

The Dame's Rocket was originally a European garden plant, but has now become an invasive plant in Michigan.

Deptford Pink

Carnation Family

aka Grass Pink

Roadsides and dry fields are home to this brilliant one half inch wide pink flower, often with tiny white spots. The Deptford Pink grows atop a stiff slender stem, eight to twenty inches tall and is accompanied by needlelike leaves.

Each plant sheds up to four hundred seeds, but it takes two years for the Deptford Pink to flower, forming only a rosette of leaves the first year after seeds are dispersed in late summer.

Some resources state that the name comes from the town Deptford in England, where the plant grew in abundance.

Downy Yellow Violet

Violet Family

aka Common Yellow Violet, Smooth Yellow Violet [2]

One characteristic that distinguishes the Downy Yellow Violet from other yellow violets is the hairiness of the heart shaped leaves. The stem is also hairy and supports both blossoms and leaves, which also differs from other yellow violets. The structure of the Downy Yellow Violet is similar to that of the Canada Violet (pp. 20-21).

The Downy Yellow Violet stands from six to sixteen inches tall; taller than many of the other early spring violets. It is found in woodlands, and along stream banks, but rarely out in the open.

When the seed capsule dries it bursts, shooting seeds in all directions, thus building small colonies of the Downy Yellow Violet.

2 Some sources state that this violet is also called Common Yellow Violet, and/or Smooth Yellow Violet, while other sources list them as separate species. Since violets intergrade, plants may be produced with intermediate characteristics, and are no longer considered separate species.

Dragon's Mouth

Orchid Family

aka Dragonmouth, Arethusa, Swamp Pink [3]

This bright two inch magenta flower with touches of yellow and white, is most often found growing in a bog. Arethusa is an appropriate alternate name, as it is the name of a river nymph of Greek mythology.

Dragon's Mouth grows in acidic sphagnum moss bogs for only a few weeks beginning the first part of June. It is located at the end of a four to twelve inch stalk which is leafless during flowering time.

The unusual lip of the flower serves as a platform for insects, but bees learn to ignore this brightly colored and sweet smelling flower as it does not produce nectar. Only inexperienced bees continue to pollinate the Dragon's Mouth.

3 Although identified as Swamp Pink by some sources, there is another flower named Swamp Pink which also grows in bogs and is a deep magenta color, but part of the Lily Family rather than the Orchid Family.

Dutchman's Breeches

Fumitory Family

aka "boys"

Although similar to Squirrel Corn (pp.106-107) this waxy white flower has a yellow tip, is odorless, and the inflated spurs suggest upside down pants. Both of these flowers are found in rich deciduous woods, but Dutchman's Breeches are more common in Michigan.

Although the fine fern-like leaves grow to about a foot tall, each individual flower is only about three fourths inch long and is in bloom a very short time.

Sometimes there is a small hole at the base of an individual flower, as bees whose proboscises are too short to reach the length of the flower, snip a hole so they can enjoy the nectar.

Fringed Polygala
Milkwort Family

aka Gaywings, Gay Wings, Fringed Milkwort, Bird-on-the-Wing, Flowering Wintergreen

The Fringed Polygala is a low-growing plant, only about three inches tall, found mainly in pine forests or rich moist woods in May and early June. The flower, which occasionally is all white, is about three fourths inch long and perches above the evergreen leaves.

This native plant is often mistaken for an orchid. Although the Milkwort Family is known for its oddly shaped flowers, the other three plants from the Milkwort Family that may be found in Michigan are vastly different from the Fringed Polygala.

This unique flower is sometimes described as a tiny airplane without a tail.

Goat's Rue
Pea Family

aka Devil's Shoestring, Rabbitpea, American Garden Rue, Catgut

The Goat's Rue begins to bloom in May, with up to two hundred small flowers atop a one to two foot stem, which is covered with silky silver hairs.

Some sources state this is a native plant, while others report that it was brought in from Europe and Eastern Asia as a food for goats to increase milk production; before it was found to contain pesticides.

The Goat's Rue emits a faint but pleasant aroma which attracts bees for nectar, but when bruised gives off a very disagreeable odor.

The stringy roots found in the sandy soil in which it grows could have initiated the name of Devil's Shoestrings.

Golden Alexanders
Carrot Family

Golden Alexanders stand one to three feet high in wet meadows, thickets, and swamps; areas where ferns normally grow. The leaflets are up to thirteen inches long, pointed, and are divided and finely cut, appearing "fern-like."

The tiny yellowish to green flowers grow in flat-topped two inch umbels, and can be found in April and May.

The Meadow Parsnip and other yellow flowered members of the Carrot Family are also referred to as Golden Alexander.

Golden Ragwort
Aster Family

aka Golden Groundsel, Butterweed, Squaw Weed

The Golden Ragwort, which grows over two feet high and has one inch daisy-like flowers in umbels, is seen in fields and along roadsides in May.

The Golden Ragwort is similar to other ragworts, but is distinguished by the small rosette of heart shaped basal leaves which are dark green on top and purple underneath.

When the flowers age, the petals curl back to form slender tubes. The seeds produced have tufts of white hairs which help them to be distributed by the wind. The roots can also spread and form colonies.

Butterflies, small bees, and flies are attracted to the Golden Ragwort, but the toxins it produces are poisonous to livestock.

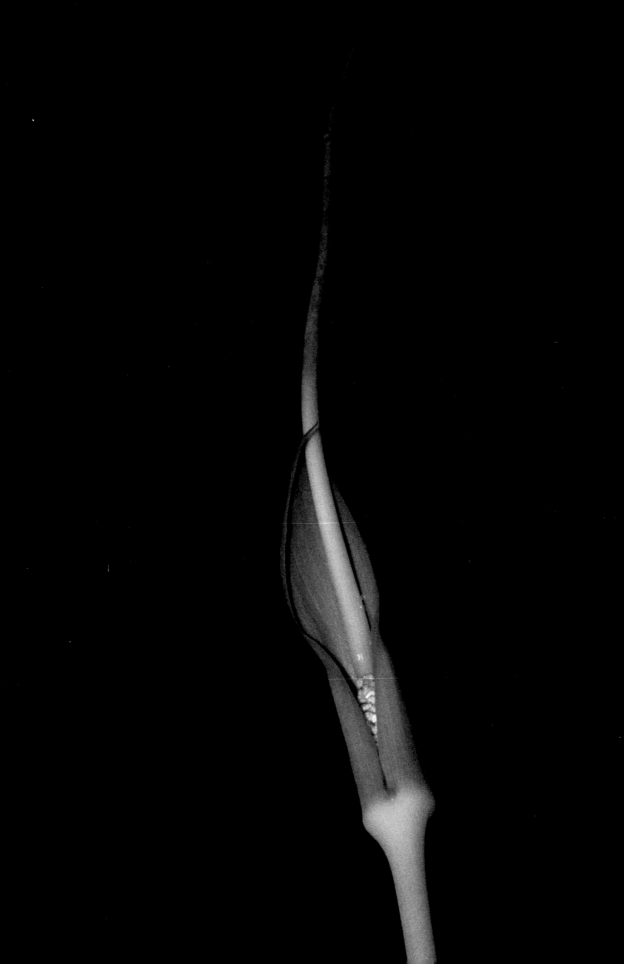

Green Dragon

Arum Family

aka Dragon Arum

The one to four foot high Green Dragon, is found in wet woodlands in May, in areas that might also be inhabited by the more common member of the Arum Family, the Jack-in-the-Pulpit (pp. 68-69). Both prefer dappled sunlight with lots of decaying leaves.

The name, Green Dragon, clearly comes from the shape of the spadix which is six to twelve inches long and looks like a dragon's tongue. The true flowers are actually the tiny greenish yellow ones at the base of the spadix.

The Green Dragon, which is quite rare, is found under large leaves which grow parallel to the ground. Its fruit looks like a green corn cob which in the fall turns a bright orange red, similar to the Water Arum (pp. 120-121) and the Jack-in-the-Pulpit.

Ground Ivy
Mint Family

aka Gill-over-the Ground, Hedgemaids, Creeping Charlie

Ground Ivy, with its one half-inch blue/purple flowers, can be found in lawns and disturbed soil beginning in April. It was imported from Europe as a ground cover and quickly takes over large areas as it branches from a creeping stem.

Ground Ivy has a square stem with opposite scalloped rounded leaves which is common to plants in the Mint Family. Crushing the highly scented leaves will also identify Ground Ivy as a member of this family.

Gill in French means "to ferment." The leaves of the Ground Ivy were once used to help flavor (ferment) beer.

Heal-all

Mint Family

aka Self Heal, All Heal

The Heal-all is a very common flower found May through September in fields, waste places, and lawns. Heal-all has the typical square stem of the Mint Family, and an odor of mint when leaves are crushed. These plants can grow six to twelve inches high if left undisturbed.

The small half-inch flowers with the upper arched lip and the lower fringed and drooping lip grow amidst the hairy bracts.

Heal-all is widely used as an herbal remedy for problems such as throat illnesses.

Hedge Bindweed
Morning Glory Family

There are numerous bindweeds, most on three to ten foot twining vines with funnel shaped flowers about two inches wide, but the Hedge Bindweed is identified by the white stripe found in pale to bright pink flowers.

Beginning in May, this flower creeps up into bushes or small trees. This plant is difficult to remove unless the roots are removed. The Hedge Bindweed is found in moist soil, along streams, roadsides, and waste places.

As its family name suggests, this flower opens in the mornings with the sun.

Henbit

Mint Family

As is characteristic of the Mint Family, the stem
of the Henbit is square and green and becomes
purple with age. The leaves are scalloped and
clasp the stem at the top, and the fine hairs that
cover the plant point downward. The Henbit does
not, however, have a strong mint scent like most
plants in the Mint Family.

The small two lipped orchid-like flower is about
one half inch long and grows four to sixteen
inches high beginning late March in waste places,
fields, and roadsides.

Chickens seem to like to eat this plant, hence the
name. Hummingbirds also like its nectar. Henbit
can be consumed fresh, or cooked and used in teas.

The Henbit reproduces solely by each plant
producing two thousand or more seeds. The Red
Henbit differs only in that its flower is red.

Hepatica
Buttercup Family

aka Liverleaf; Liverwort

In the spring, two types of Hepaticas, barely distinguishable except for the leaf lobes and bracts of the plants, can be found. Both plants have similar three fourths inch flowers, can occur in the same woods, and may hybridize, making exact identification of the Round-lobed Hepatica and the Sharp-lobed Hepatica very difficult.

This native flower begins to decorate the forest floor as early as April and grows four to six inches tall. As the stems lengthen and droop toward the ground, ants collect and disperse the seeds.

Hepatica comes from the Greek word hepar, which refers to the liver. Early herbalists used this plant to treat liver disease, as an appetite stimulant, and as a tonic.

Herb Robert

Geranium Family

aka Robert Geranium, Stinky Bob, Red Robin

The Herb Robert, found in May in the woods, and along shores, are shades of pink and sometimes white. It is a small flower, only about one half inch, growing close to the ground. The plant is covered with short glandular hairs, giving it a sticky feeling, and a distinct odor when the leaves are crushed.

Similarities can be found to the Wild Geranium (pp. 128-129), another member of the Geranium Family, which blossoms about the same time as the Herb Robert.

Some states have labeled this European import a noxious weed, because it is a fast- growing ground cover and displaces native plants.

Hoary Alyssum
Mustard Family

The Hoary Alyssum is one of more than three thousand species of mustards, identified by the four petals of the flower, the grayish green hairy stems, and the many branches of flowers near the top. It is found in meadows, pastures, and hay fields, but poisonings in animals can occur if a large amount is consumed.

The Hoary Alyssum was introduced from Europe and Asia, has spread rapidly due to the high number of seeds each plant produces, and is now considered an aggressive invader.

Jack-in-the-Pulpit
Arum Family

aka Indian Turnip

The unique Jack-in-the-Pulpit has a three inch curved spathe (pulpit) which bends forward over the spadix (Jack) atop an erect stem about a foot tall.

As in all plants in the Arum Family, the actual flowers are the tiny flowers that are found on the spadix, the yellowish club shaped center.

Research of this flower shows disagreement concerning the different colors of the spathe and stem; some are a rich burgundy, and others remain a pale green. This variation may be due to different species, or the age of the plant, or the soil content.

The green seeds, about the size of a pea, form on the spadix and become a bright red by early fall.

Native Americans used the root of the Jack-in-the-Pulpit as food similar in taste to a turnip.

Large-flowered Bellwort

Lily Family

aka Perfoliate Bellflower, Merry Bells, Cowbells, Wood Daffodil

The Large-flowered Bellwort blooms for two weeks in April with the upper portion of each plant bending down, and the long petals appearing somewhat twisted. The leaves of the Large-flowered Bellwort, however, are perfoliate, as it appears the stem is growing through the leaves.

The Large-flowered Bellwort's numbers are declining due to grazing animals, especially deer, and the invasion of various non-native plants.

Bellworts have been used for medical problems including snakebites and various infections.

Large-flowered Trillium
Lily Family

aka White Flowered Trillium, Wakerobin [4]

Mid to late spring will find the forest floor covered with Large-flowered Trilliums. There are three sets of three with the Trilliums: three petals, three sepals, and three leaves.

The Large-flowered Trillium is the most common of the nine species of trilliums found in Michigan. The seeds drop to the ground, split open, and are dispersed by ants. It then takes six to eight years for the plant to mature into a flower. This flower is one of many protected flowers and should never be picked.

White-tailed Deer like to eat both the foliage and flowers of the trilliums, especially the Large-flowered Trillium because the flowers are larger and easily seen.

The waxy white petals soon turn a pale pink to show the flowers are aging.

---

4 *Wakerobin* is an alternate name for most trilliums, as they bloom when robins nest.

Leadplant
Pea Family

aka False Indigo, Downy Indigobush, Lead Plant, Prairie Shoestring

The Leadplant blooms in upland prairies for about three weeks. It is usually found in shadowy places, but tends to lean toward the sun.

Although most flowers found in the Pea Family have three petals, this one half inch flower has only one petal, which begins as a tube and then unfolds to show the red stamens and yellow anthers.

The unique name of this one to three foot high plant comes from the fine hairs on the plant that make it look like it was "dusted" with white lead. Native Americans used Leadplant leaves for smoking, and for making a tea.

Long-spurred Violet
Violet Family

The Long-spurred Violet flower is about a half inch wide, and the longer spur extends out the back of the flower. This plant is four to eight inches tall, with the flowers and the heart-shaped leaves, on the same stem. It is most often found in rich limey soil.

The Long-spurred Violet is similar to other flowers in the Violet Family and often confused with the Dog Violet. The Dog Violet, however, does not have the darker purple center of the Long-spurred Violet. The Great-spurred violet, has a short, wide spur with a rounded end, rather than the long pointed spur of the Long-spurred Violet.

Marsh Marigold
Buttercup Family

aka Fairy Cups, Cowslip [5]

The Marsh Marigold with its shiny yellow flower decorates stream edges early in the spring. The thick hollow branching stems hold the one inch flowers above standing water. The deep green glossy heart shaped leaves also help to make this a flower that is easily identified.

The Marsh Marigold spreads by reseeding itself; therefore, it is usually found in large colonies ranging in height from six inches to two feet.

True marigolds are members of the Aster Family, while the Marsh Marigold is very similar to the Large Buttercup.

5 While some sources use Cowslip as another name for Marsh Marigold, others state that it only resembles a Cowslip, which grows in fields and pastures and not in wet areas.

Mayapple
Barberry Family

aka May Apple, Devil's Apple, Duck's Foot, Ground Lemon, Indian Apple, Mandrake, Umbrella Plant

The Mayapple flower is found under two large umbrella-like leaves. This waxy, nodding flower is about two inches across with six to nine petals and is found in the V of the stem.

The fruit (apple) is a pulpy lemon-yellow berry which can be used in jellies; however, the deer usually trample the leaves and eat the fruit before they can be harvested.

Native American tribes gathered the rhizomes of the Mayapple in the fall, dried them, and then ground them into a powder to treat various ailments.

The blossom of the Mayapple is similar to an apple blossom which also blooms in May, which may account for the name of this plant.

Miterwort

Saxifuge Family

aka Bishop's Cap

The Miterwort has very tiny flowers, about one eighth inch wide with five delicately fringed petals on a stem about eight inches tall. Due to its size, it is easy to miss the Miterwort among many other larger flowers blooming in the rich woods in April.

The fruit of the Miterwort is the shape of a bishop's small cap called a miter.

Another common Miterwort in Michigan is the Naked Miterwort, which has larger greenish yellow flowers and fewer leaves.

Northern Pitcher-plant

Pitcher-plant Family

The Northern Pitcher-plant can be found in sphagnum bogs beginning in May. Easily identified from a distance, the eight to twenty-four inch tall, leafless stalk has one large dark red droopy flower about two inches wide.

The Northern Pitcher-plant is one of the few carnivorous plants found in Michigan. The rosette of leaves, which are reddish green with obvious veins, hollow and inflated, collect water and insects. The inner surface of the leaf is covered with hairs that point downward, which makes it difficult for insects to escape from the leaves. The insects are digested by the enzymes in the rainwater and give the plant its needed nutrients.

Pink Lady's Slipper
Orchid Family

aka Pink Moccasin Flower

Pink Lady's Slipper, one of the largest orchids in Michigan, standing around a foot tall, is two inches long, and can be found under pines, oaks, or red maples. It has an inflated deep pink lower petal with red veins, fading to a pale pink as it ages. The upper petals are long and narrow.

A Pink Lady's Slipper can live to be twenty or more years old, but it needs help from larger bees. It takes a strong insect to get inside this sweet smelling flower because the flower is closed. Once inside, the bee realizes that there is no nectar, but while trying to get out it becomes covered with pollen. As the bee repeats this with other Pink Lady's Slipper, it spreads the pollen, thus helping to make new seeds.

The Pink Lady's Slipper is an endangered species due to the seven year span from seed to flowering.

Prickly Pear
Cactus Family

The Prickly Pear flower accompanies flat, fleshy, green pads covered with reddish brown barbed bristles. The plants seen in Michigan grow close to the ground, and spread over a wide area.

Other species of the Cactus Family, such as the Plains Prickly Pear and the Fragile Prickly Pear can also be found in Michigan, but the reddish center of this plant identifies it as simply, Prickly Pear.

Prickly Pear is commercially used in jellies, candies, juices, teas, and alcoholic drinks. The Native Americans used its juice to treat burns and diabetes.

Purple Trillium

Lily Family

aka Stinking Benjamin, Red Trillium, Wake-robin, Stinking Willie

The Purple Trillium, with a slightly drooping blossom, is found in rich woods, most often on the far eastern coast of Michigan.

The Purple Trillium maintains most of the characteristics of other trilliums such as the three leaves, petals, and sepals, and its maroon or reddish brown color is similar to the Toadshade (pp.116-117). The leaves are web veined, rather than parallel veined like most flowers in the Lily Family.

Its unpleasant odor, similar to a wet dog, attracts the carrion flies which pollinate this particular trillium.

Indians used the Purple Trillium root as a medicinal aid during childbirth.

Rabbit-foot Clover

Pea Family

aka Pussy Clover

Rabbit-foot Clover is four to sixteen inches tall with a fuzzy round to cylindrical flower head about one inch long. The actual flowers are tiny white to pale pink pea-shaped flowers hidden amongst the feathery pink to gray calyx. Bees suck the nectar from these hidden flowers.

The leaflets are less than one inch wide and are toothed at the tips only.

Rabbit-foot Clover is usually found in dry open sites beginning in May, but can still be seen as late as October in some areas. The flowers are annuals and each year new plants sprout from reseeding.

Rough-fruited Cinquefoil

Rose Family

aka Sulfur Cinquefoil

The Rough-fruited Cinquefoil is found in fields and along roadsides in full sun from May through July. It is easily identifiable among the many roadside plants as it stands about two feet tall and has flat topped clusters of heart-shaped petals.

The Rough-fruited Cinquefoil is native to Europe and Asia, but is now considered a problem weed in most places where it has been introduced.

The Rough-fruited Cinquefoil is one of many cinquefoils found in Michigan, with all others being a dark golden yellow.

Rue Anemone

Buttercup Family

aka Windflower

The early blooms of the Rue Anemone are found in large groups in wet shady deciduous woods. The green center and the seven to nine petals help to distinguish the Rue Anemone from other small white spring flowers.

The Rue Anemone is a delicate plant with two to three flowers on slender stalks above a whorl of three lobed leaves. It takes just a small breeze to move this flower, thus its alternative name, windflower.

The Rue Anemone is easily confused with False Rue Anemone as well as Wood Anemone. The False Rue Anemone has multiple flowers but each has only five petals. Wood Anemone; however, has only one flower per plant with five petals (pp. 132–133).

Showy Lady's-slipper
Orchid Family

aka Pink-and-white Lady's Slipper

The Showy Lady's-slipper, blooming late May, is considered by many to be the most beautiful of the northern native orchids, and definitely the largest. Each flower is about three inches long with one blossom to a stem being the norm.

The Showy Lady's Slipper can be found in spruce bogs, tamarack bogs, swamps, wet meadows, and prairies throughout Michigan. It will survive the longest where there is damp ground and lots of sun.

Extreme caution should be used around this flower as it takes up to seven years for the root system and the first leaves to develop, and up to fifteen years before the first blooms are seen. Once developed, some plants are reported to have had a lifespan of one hundred years.

The hairy leaves and stems of the Showy Lady's-slipper are extremely poisonous to some people, causing a reaction similar to that of Poison Ivy.

Solomon's Seal

Lily Family

aka True Solomon Seal

Michigan has three very similar species of Solomon's Seal with bell shaped flowers hanging beneath the leaves on an arching stem. All three grow well in partial sun, from April to about June, in wooded areas where the soil is rich.

The Smooth and Hairy species are nearly identical except Hairy Solomon's Seal has minute hairs on the undersides of the leaves. The Smooth Solomon's Seal leaf is smooth on both sides, and both are clearly parallel-veined. Berries from both species are pea size and vary from blackish blue to purple and red.

The Great Solomon's Seal may be twice as large as the other species, with two to ten bell shaped flowers per cluster hanging beneath the leaves.

The Solomon's Seal varies from the Starflowered Solomon's Seal, whose flowers form a spike at the end of the plant rather than hanging below the stem (pp. 112–113).

Spiderwort
Spiderwort Family

The Spiderwort is about two feet tall with fifteen-inch leaves that appear folded lengthwise forming a groove, similar to an Iris leaf. The deep purple, and sometimes white flower, is found in a terminal cluster.

An intriguing part of this flower is the "hair" in the center of the flower. It is reported that this is a chain of thin-walled cells, and the flowing cytoplasm and nucleus can be seen under a microscope.

The one to two inch flowers bloom in the morning, but rather than fall off, they disintegrate through a plant enzyme into a jelly-like fluid. The leaf, when torn apart, becomes stringy like a spider web.

From April through June this unique plant can be found in open woods or on roadsides.

Spring Beauty
Purslane Family

aka Virginia Spring Beauty, Fairy Spuds

The Spring Beauty is a six to ten inch tall flower that is only open on warm, sunny days. When closed the flower nods downward to protect itself.

The showy Spring Beauty is less than an inch wide, with fine pink stripes on the white petals guiding the insects into the yellow tinted center to find the nectar. This pink stripe can be very pale to very bright.

This native flower reseeds itself, and thus soon develops large patches of flowers in the deciduous forests. Thin tapered leaves accompany this flower.

Colonists and Native Americans ate the small tubers that have a sweet chestnut flavor.

Squirrel Corn

Fumitory Family

aka "girls"

Although the fernlike foliage of the Squirrel Corn is very similar to that of the Dutchman's Breeches, the bloom is quite different. This flower has the nickname "girls" as the flower is heart shaped, lacking the long spurs (pants) of the Dutchman's Breeches (pp. 42-43).

Squirrel Corn flowers are often found with holes in the side where insects have sucked out the nectar, due to the length of the spur.

The name Squirrel Corn comes from the shape of the tubers, which resemble corn kernels.

Squirrel Corn is very fragrant with a hyacinth scent, but due to the alkaloids in the plant it is very poisonous to cattle.

Star Chickweed

Carnation Family

aka Starweed, Starwort

The Star Chickweed is found in April and May and is the showiest of the dozen or more chickweeds found in Michigan. The petals surround a pearl like center and form a beautiful one half-inch star. Although it has five petals, it appears to have ten due to the deep clefts in each petal. Unique to this chickweed are the long anthers with the brown ends.

The chickweeds can be eaten as a salad green and is a favorite food of chickens and wild birds.

Another common chickweed found in May is the Mouse-ear Chickweed, with clefts that are not as deep as the Star Chickweed, and stems and leaves that have sticky hairs.

Starflower
Primrose Family

The Starflower blooms for a short time in May, in shade, in both conifer and deciduous woods, and is a relatively fragile plant. It stands six to twelve inches tall, and is unique in that it normally has seven petals, a number of petals not common in the plant world. One or two "stars" are on thin stems above a whorl of five to seven long, shiny, tapered leaves. These leaves are stalk less and very finely toothed.

The Starflower is a perennial herb that grows from slender, creeping rhizomes. It is pollinated by native bees and goes dormant in midsummer. The yellow leaves fall to the ground, leaving just a stem with one or two tiny seed capsules ripening at the top.

Star-flowered Solomon's Seal
Lily Family

aka Starry Solomon's-plume, Starry False Solomon's Seal

Star-flowered Solomon's Seal has tiny flowers which make up a spike cluster at the end of a zigzag arching stem, rather than hanging below like the Solomon's Seals (pp. 100-101). It is similar to the False Solomon's Seal, but the False Solomon's Seal has a larger flower than that of the Star-flowered Solomon's Seal, and the flower cluster is smaller. Both species have parallel veins on leaves that clasp the zigzag stem.

The Star-flowered Solomon's Seal is found mainly in moist wet woodlands from May through June, with the fruit (berries) changing from off-white with dark strips to solid blackish red when fully ripe in August.

Teaberry
Heath Family

aka Wintergreen

The Teaberry evergreen leaf is waxy and leathery, roundish, and about one to two inches wide. The one third inch white bellshaped nodding flower begins to bloom in April. The petals are fused together to form the bell, with one to three flowers per plant.

Small colonies of these plants are formed due to the creeping underground stems.

The red berries that form in the summer are enjoyed by birds, wildlife, and hikers, due to their sweet taste.

Teaberry extract is used to flavor teas, candies, medicines, and chewing gum, with a wintergreen flavor.

Toadshade

Lily Family

aka Toad Trillium, Sessile Trillium

The Toadshade is a four to twelve inch tall trillium, with the standard three petals, but unlike other trilliums these one and a half inch long petals remain erect and appear to be closed. This is the only sessile flowered Trillium growing in Michigan.

The leaves, although maintaining the whorl right below the flower, are very large and mottled.

The Toadshade is found in April in very rich woods that have never been cleared. The extreme southwestern corner of the state is one known location of this species in Michigan.

It is not unusual to smell an odor similar to that of decaying flesh in the vicinity of this plant, especially on warm days.

Trout Lily
Lily Family

aka Adder's Tongue, Dogtooth Violet, Fawn Lily, Serpent's Tongue, Yellow Snowdrop

The leaves of the Trout Lily are some of the first green seen in the spring on the forest floor. The mottling of the leaves resembles the Brown or Brook Trout, thus its name.

The flowers, which are bronze on the outside, open only during the day. The Trout Lily is one of the most common spring flowers and is found in large colonies. The two leaves and a bloom represent a mature plant.

Although yellow is the most common color of Trout Lilies in Michigan, a few White Trout Lilies grow within the patches of the yellow ones.

Trout Lilies are pollinated by ants, and it then takes seven years for these seeds to become a tuber or bulb and to produce flowers.

Native Americans made the greens of the Trout Lily into stews, and also used the greens for treatment of ulcers and vomiting.

Water Arum

Arum Family

aka Wild Calla, Wild Water Lily

The Water Arum begins to bloom near the end of May and can be found in bogs and pond edges, rising about six inches above the water surface.

As is common in the Arum Family, the actual flowers are the tiny yellow flowers found on a one inch long spadix, which is clasped by a white spathe about two inches long.

Water Arum leaves are heart-shaped, smooth, and shiny, and are on separate stalks which arise from the base of the plant.

Its fruit is a cluster of small green berries which turn red in the late summer, similar to others in the Arum Family (pp. 52–53 and 68-69).

Wild Blue Flax

Flax Family

aka Lewis Flax, Prairie Flax

The one to two foot tall stems of the Wild Blue Flax are grey or bluish green with eight to ten blossoms. These blue one inch flowers, veined in darker blue, bloom from the bottom of the stem up to the top.

The Wild Blue Flax can be found during May and June on prairies and plains, but the short lived flowers open only during the early morning hours and close by noon.

Although the stems appear to be slender and fragile they are actually fibrous and tough and were used by Native Americans for cords and similar items. Wild Blue Flax is related to Common Flax, from which linen and linseed oil is made. Domestic or Common Flax has a white blossom as opposed to the blue of the Wild Blue Flax.

Wild Blue Phlox

Phlox Family

aka Wild Sweet William

Before the Wild Blue Phlox flowers open in April, the closed buds have twisted petals like a torch. Phlox means "flame" in Greek, thus the name. When open, the three fourth inch flowers form a loose flat cluster atop a sticky, hairy stem. The Wild Blue Phlox, found in the eastern states, including Michigan, have notched petals, which differs from those found in the Western states.

The fragrant Wild Blue Phlox stands ten to twenty inches tall, and is most common in wet shady woods and fields.

Wild Four O'Clocks

Four-o'clock Family

aka Heart-leaved four-o'clock, Heart-leaved Umbrellawort

As the name suggests, Wild Four O'Clocks open in late afternoon and remain open at night. A cluster of one half-inch flowers form atop tall, smooth, slightly angled stems.

The green bracts form a star-shaped cup which opens to expose the flowers. After the flower blooms, the bracts expand during seed production and become a parachute for seed distribution.

The magenta petals with bright yellow filaments have little to no fragrance.

Wild Geranium

Geranium Family

aka Cranesbill [6]

The Wild Geranium is one of the first brightly colored flowers of spring amidst all the pastels and whites. The plants grow one to two feet high and the blossoms about two inches wide.

The Wild Geranium is found mainly in the southern half of the Lower Peninsula in shady woods or meadows.

The name Cranesbill refers to the elongated pistil which becomes the seed pod and looks like the bill of a crane. The seeds pop from this long capsule and can fly several yards, thus forming large colonies of flowers in an area.

Native Americans ground the dried rhizomes into powder to stop bleeding and to make a medicine for sore throats.

6 Cranesbill is an alternate name for numerous Geraniums due to the common seed pod shape within this family.

Wild Lupine
Pea Family

The Wild Lupine is most often found in May in the southern half of Michigan's lower peninsula, along roadsides and in meadows. The plant stands one to two feet high, with the five-eighths-inch pea-like flowers forming a spike.

Lupus in Latin stands for wolf, and lupines were once thought to "wolf" the mineral content of the soil. Actually, all plants in the pea family enhance soil fertility.

American Indians used a cold tea made from the leaves to treat nausea.

The Wild Lupine is a host plant for the Karner Blue Butterfly caterpillar, which is a threatened species in Michigan.

Wood Anemone

Buttercup Family

aka Mayflower, Nightcaps, Windflower

The star like flower of the Wood Anemone is an early spring flower. Leaflets wrap around the flower bud before it unfolds. As night or rain approaches the flower closes and hangs down so it won't be damaged.

The Wood Anemone takes up to five years to bloom. Its very thin stalk moves easily in the breeze and is sometimes called a Windflower because of this. The Greek word for wind is anemos.

The Wood Anemone is similar to the Rue Anemone (pp. 96-97) although the Rue Anemone has numerous flowers atop each stalk, while Wood Anemone has only one flower.

Yellow Lady's Slipper

Orchid Family

There are two species of Yellow Lady's Slippers found throughout Michigan: the Large and the Small. Besides size, they are similar in appearance, both producing an inflated yellow pouch lip petal. The spirally twisted greenish-yellow to brownish-purple structures are the upper petals.

The Yellow Lady's Slipper, whose Latin name means "a little shoe," blooms for about three weeks in bogs, swamps, and deciduous woods beginning in April.

Cherokee Indians used the roots to make a treatment for worms.

As with most Lady's Slippers, it takes five to eight years for this plant to grow from seed to flower, so it should never be uprooted, moved, or picked.

AUTHOR'S NOTES

This book is not meant to be a flower identification book, but rather an opportunity for the reader to view each wildflower, isolated and up close, and to enjoy the intricacies and uniqueness of each flower. Taking time to look closely at each photo, however, will assist the reader in recognizing the flowers when seen again while walking along a wooded path or through a meadow, or driving down a highway. The narratives are informational pieces about what makes each plant unique. For those who want more in-depth information, I encourage them to utilize the References in the next pages.

Due to the size of our beautiful state of Michigan, the same wildflower may bloom in the south in April, but not until June in northern portions of Michigan. In choosing which flowers should appear in which book, I tried to choose the time they most often bloomed in the central part of the state. Depending on the winter, the weather, the amount of nitrogen in the air from summer storms, a flower may appear in May one year and in June in the same location the next year; therefore, categorizing flowers into Spring, Early Summer, or Late Summer volumes was my best guess based on years of discovery.

Spelling of wildflowers and placements in families differ according to publication, so I have used the most recent National Audubon Society Field Guide to North American Wildflowers: Eastern, copyright 2001, as the determining reference.

ABOUT THE AUTHOR
DR. DEE HOWE

As a child, I discovered the beauty of Michigan through walks in the forests, playing in the wooded areas around my home, biking to friends' houses with stops to explore the bits of color along the road and in the fields. I joined a Michigan Wildflowers 4-H Club to learn more. I learned to look closely at the number and shape of the petals and leaves, to count the pistils and stamens, to note how the leaves were attached to the stems, and more. I learned some names of the flowers, but more importantly I learned to appreciate the unique beauty of the very small intricate violets, as well as the large bold lilies.

Through college, raising children, career moves, whenever I found the need to escape from the craziness of the world, I would head to the woods to walk and explore. Walking amongst the trees, observing the flowers, the butterflies, listening to the stillness, or the sounds of birds brings me a peacefulness that I have not been able to find elsewhere.

About twenty years ago I decided that it would be nice to capture some of these images in the woods so I purchased new Nikon. Trial and error led to many rolls of film being printed. When visiting my father one day, he said, "Why don't you do something with all those pictures you are taking. Here is a photography show you can enter." I did, and was called a couple days later and was told that this show was not for professionals, only amateurs were allowed to compete. Since this was the first time I had ever shown any of my photos, I let them know that I considered myself an amateur! This was the validation I needed that maybe, just maybe, I could capture a bit of the beauty I had so enjoyed throughout my life to share with others.

For the next few years I was out in the woods every chance I had. I'd throw a cooler in the back of the car, fill my pockets with film, and away I would go. It would take me all day to travel ten miles as I constantly stopped to explore a flower that caught my eye, and then a little farther down the path there would be a different flower, and then, there's another one over under that tree.....

I began to think about how I could share these photos with a larger audience and this series of books, Michigan Wildflowers: Up Close and Personal, came to be.

GLOSSARY

axils the angle where the stem and leaf meet

basal leaves leaves at the base of the plant

beards a tuft of long and/or stiff hairs

bract leaf at the base of the flower, usually small

calyx the outside set of petals usually green but can be colored

conifer plants/trees that do not shed their leaves

deciduous plants/trees that shed their leaves

hybridize crossbreed between two species of plants

lobed indentations on the leaf that don't meet the center

node the area on a stem where a leaf or root grows

pistil the female organ of a flower

rosette a round cluster of leaves that seem to grow right out of the ground

sessile when the leaf is attached directly to the stem

spadix a thick spike of dense flowers

spathe bract that encloses the flower

spur a projection from a flower that is usually hollow

stamen the male organ of the flower

umbel a flower cluster where all the flower stalks grow from the same point

whorl a circle of three or more leaves

SELECTED RESOURCES

Books

Barker, J. *A Pocket Guide to Wild Flowers of North America*.
China: Parragon, 2009

Brown, P. *Wild Orchids of the Northeastern United States*.
Ithaca, New York: Comstock Publishing Associates, 1993

Case, F. *Orchids of the Western Great Lakes Region*.
Michigan: Cranbrook Institute of Science, 1987.

Case, F. and Case, R. *Trilliums*.
Portland: Timber Press, 1997

Courtenay, B. and Zimmerman, J. *Wildflowers and Weeds*.
New York: Prentice Hall Press, 1978.

Hausman, E. *The Illustrated Encyclopedia of American Wildflowers*.
New York: Garden City Publishing Co., Inc., 1947.

Lund, H. *Michigan Wildflowers*.
Michigan: Altwerger & Mandel Publishing Co., 1992.

National Audubon Society. *Field Guide to North American Wildflowers: Eastern Region*. New York: Alfred A. Knopf, 2001.

Peterson Field Guide. *Wildflowers: Northeastern/Northcentral North America*.
Boston: Houghton Mifflin Company.

Stokes, D. and Stokes, L. *The Wildflower Book*.
Boston: Little, Brown and Company, 1992.

Tekiela, S. *Wildflowers of Michigan*.
Cambridge, Minnesota: Adventure Publications, Inc., 2000.

Websites

http://2bnthewild.com

http://gnps.org

http://plants.usda.gov

http://wildflowers.jdcc.edu

http://www.araagriculture.org

http://www.ashevillenatural.com

http://www.blueplanetbiomes.org

http://www.botany.wisc.edu

http://www.briartech.com

http://www.britannica.com

http://www.ces.ncsu.edu

http://www.chicagobotanic.org

http://www.dnr.state.mn.us

http://www.fs.fed.us/wildflower

http://www.fws.gov

http://www.fws.gov/Midwest/Endangered/plants

http://www.gpnc.org

http://www.hort.purdue.edu

http://www.illinoiswildflowers.info

http://www.inhs.uiuc.edu

http://www.invasive.org

http://www.michigan.gov/dnr

http://www.minnesotawildflowers.info

http://www.newhampshirewildflowers.com

http://www.nps.gov

http://www.npwrc.usgs.gov

http://www.oardc.ohio-state.edu

http://www.rootcellar.us/wildflowers

http://www.wildflower.org

https://gobotany.newenglandwild.org

Have you wondered what is that little purple flower growing in your lawn? Or the tall yellow one growing alongside the road? Have you just not found the time to dig through field guides to identify them or to learn more about them?

Michigan Wildflowers: Up Close and Personal is focused on just the spring wildflowers found in Michigan and photographed with a unique perspective. To quote Georgia O'Keffee, "A flower is relatively small. Everyone has many associations with a flower... but nobody sees a flower — really ... I'll paint it big and they will be surprised into taking time to look at it." These close-ups reflect that philosophy and will allow people to experience wildflowers in a way they haven't before.

$23.99
ISBN 978-1-939556-22-6
52399>

PenCraft Books

9 781939 556226

INDEX OF MICHIGAN WILDFLOWERS

Check other Michigan Wildflower books by Dr. Dee Howe

Michigan Wildflowers: Up Close and Personal
Early Summer Volume

— and —

Michigan Wildflowers: Up Close and Personal
Late Summer Volume

ABOUT
PENCRAFT BOOKS, LLC

PenCraft Books, *your* ally in fulfilling *your* dream.

Stress Relief:

We created PenCraft Books because the learning curve that we had to overcome, as authors ourselves, was so steep and so totally unrelated to finishing the book and successfully selling the book in the marketplace. The stress of figuring out how to get the book finished was intense enough without having to learn new skills to get the book into the various formats for online reading and hardcopy versions, to select the correct distribution channels, to organize the marketing of the finished book.

Authors Asked For:

We talked with many authors and discovered a common theme...Authors need some support...otherwise all authors are really working by themselves...isolated and alone. The authors indicated that they need three types of support:

1. Personal Mentor: they *wished they'd had a personal mentor when they first started writing*. Someone who cared and had the expertise to guide them along the path from original idea; to beating the dreaded procrastination, overcoming limiting self-beliefs right through to seeing their work in print. Essentially, we help them become authors and achieve a finished manuscript.
2. Marketing: It's said that *writing a book is the easy part; it's the marketing of it when the real work starts.* That's why PenCraft helps its authors stand out in a crowded market place with a marketing strategy to reach the widest possible audience and achieve maximum sales.
3. Publishing: they wished they could simply turn this process over to someone who could get the book published without the inherent stress. PenCraft prepares the finished manuscripts so they're available for readers both physically in bookstores, and on-line.

PenCraft, *your* coach in publishing *your* book...to help you reach *your* dream of writing your book

www.PenCraftBooks.com